11/03

20.95

HERNANDO DE SOTO
and the Spanish Search for Gold in World History

Titles *in World History*

HERNANDO DE SOTO
and the Spanish Search for Gold in World History

Ann Graham Gaines

Enslow Publishers, Inc.

40 Industrial Road   PO Box 38
Box 398   Aldershot
Berkeley Heights, NJ 07922 Hants GU12 6BP
USA   UK

http://www.enslow.com

Library of Congress Cataloging-in-Publication Data

Gaines, Ann.
    Hernando de Soto and the Spanish search for gold in world history /
Ann Graham Gaines.
      p. cm. — (In world history)
Includes bibliographical references (p.) and index.
    ISBN 0-7660-1821-0
    1. Soto, Hernando de, ca. 1500–1542—Juvenile literature. 2.
Explorers—America—Biography—Juvenile literature. 3. Explorers—
Spain—Biography—Juvenile literature. 4. America—Discovery and
exploration—Spanish—Juvenile literature. 5. Southern States—Discovery
and exploration—Spanish—Juvenile literature. 6. Mississippi River—
Discovery and exploration—Spanish—Juvenile literature. I. Title. II.
Series.
    E125.S7 G05 2002
    970.01′6′092—dc21
                                   2001001975

Printed in the United States of America

10 9 8 7 6 5 4 3 2

To Our Readers: We have done our best to make sure all Internet addresses in this
book were active and appropriate when we went to press. However, the author
and the publisher have no control over and assume no liability for the material
available on those Internet sites or on other Web sites they may link to. Any
comments or suggestions can be sent by e-mail to comments@enslow.com or to
the address on the back cover.

Illustration Credits: Enslow Publishers, Inc., pp. 6, 50, 58, 100; Library of
Congress, pp. 10, 12, 17, 23, 28, 31, 32, 34, 37, 44, 60, 62, 63, 69, 75, 76, 78, 81,
82, 87, 92, 94, 97.

Cover Illustration: © Digital Vision Ltd. (Background Map); Library of
Congress (De Soto Portrait)

Contents

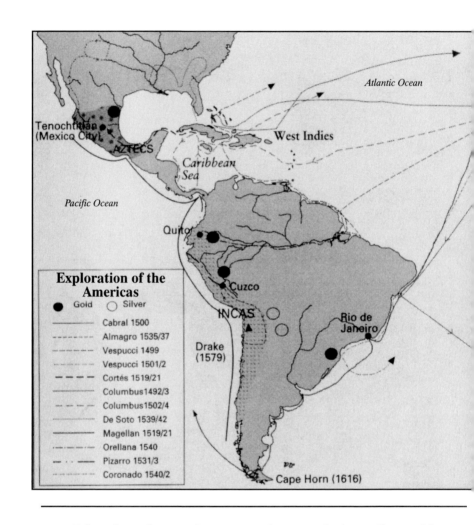

Exploration of the Americas

- ● Gold   ○ Silver

- ———— Cabral 1500
- ‑‑‑‑‑ Almagro 1535/37
- ———— Vespucci 1499
- ———— Vespucci 1501/2
- ‑ ‑ ‑ ‑ Cortés 1519/21
- ———— Columbus 1492/3
- ‑ ‑ ‑ Columbus 1502/4
- ———— De Soto 1539/42
- ———— Magellan 1519/21
- ‑ · ‑ · ‑ Orellana 1540
- ‑ · · ‑ Pizarro 1531/3
- ‑‑‑‑‑ Coronado 1540/2

Tenochtitlan (Mexico City)
AZTECS
West Indies
Caribbean Sea
Pacific Ocean
Atlantic Ocean
Quito
Cuzco
INCAS
Drake (1579)
Rio de Janeiro
Cape Horn (1616)

Fifteenth- and sixteenth-century explorers made their influence felt in all parts of the New World.

Chapter 1

The Landing

On May 25, 1539, nine Spanish ships sailed up the western coast of a land that had been named "La Florida" by explorer Ponce de Leon more than twenty years before. The expedition found the entrance to a great bay that it called the *Bahia de Espiritu Santu*. Today, it is called Tampa Bay, and more than a million people live along its tropical beaches. In 1539, there were perhaps a hundred American Indian huts along the beach. This land was unknown to the Spaniards. They had heard rumors of great treasures, fantastic animals, and springs of water to be found there that would make a person live forever.

Captain Hernando de Soto was the rich and famous Spanish conquistador (explorer who intended to conquer new lands) who had paid for the nine ships and all of the equipment they contained for a four-year expedition. His mission was supposed to be to bring the Christian religion and the benefits of European civilization to the native Americans. Of course, de Soto would not ignore riches. If the explorers found those rumored treasures—especially gold—along the way, each member of the expedition would receive a share.

For several days, Hernando de Soto and some of his best sailors searched for the safest channel to bring their heavily loaded ships into the bay. By May 28, all the ships were safely inside. On May 30, they began to unload their most valuable cargo, starting with 220 horses. Horses—unknown in North America—were an important part of any conquering mission. With the horses ashore and safe, the ships then proceeded further into the bay and off-loaded the rest of the supplies near the mouth of the Little Manatee River. More than seven hundred crew members, foot soldiers, cavalry, and even two women also went ashore. Among the supplies, which were supposed to last the Spaniards four years, were packs of war dogs and a mobile emergency food supply—herds of pigs.[1]

The five large ships returned to Cuba, while the four smaller ships remained in Tampa Bay for the expedition to use. Search parties were sent out into the countryside to gather food. Seven hundred people need a large amount of food every day just to survive. Each person could easily consume two to three pounds of food at every meal. This means that the expedition would require several tons of food every day.

But it was simply impossible for the expedition to carry more than one or two days' worth of food and supplies. They were forced to live off the land, and borrow or steal from the local Indians. They could not go where there was no food. Reliance on the local population for food also limited the expedition in another dramatic way. The local Indians stored their surplus crops so that they would have something to eat during the winter. If de Soto's expedition took these crops to eat as it passed through Indian territory, it would doom the local tribe to starvation. In order to force the Indians to give up their food, de Soto often kidnapped important members of the local tribes and held them until the Spanish expedition had passed through their territory. It was a tactic that made an enemy of the Indians and would ultimately doom the expedition to failure. At this time of the year, however, there simply was not much food to collect. In June, the first corn crop was just ripening in central Florida. De Soto knew that his crew would have to move on quickly.

Besides food, there was one other thing that de Soto needed desperately—a way to communicate with the local Indian tribes along the expedition route. None of the Spaniards could speak any of the local Indian languages. This led to some hostile encounters between the Spanish and the Indians.

One day, a search party looking for food and information came to a village after crossing a swampy area. When the people of the village saw the oncoming Spaniards, they ran away and dived into a nearby river

The Spaniards were sometimes rumored to hunt Indians for sport.

to escape. The Spaniards managed to capture four women and were in the process of taking them back to de Soto when they were attacked by the Indians.

The fight between the Spaniards on foot and the Indians was an even match. The Indians were very nimble and could fire their bows and arrows while moving in a crouched position that made it very difficult for the Spaniards to hit them with their crossbows and arquebuses (shotguns). The Indians would flee when the Spaniards approached with their steel swords, for which their war clubs were no match, but when the Spaniards turned back, the Indians would once again follow and attack. In this way, the Indians were able to kill one Spaniard and wound five others.

The Spaniards went around the swamp in circles for the rest of the day. The situation looked bleak for

Source Document

The Spaniards with their Horses, their Speares and Lances, began to commit murders, and strange cruelties: they entred into Townes, Borowes, and Villages, sparing neither children nor old men, neither women with childe, neither them that lay in, but that they ripped their bellies, and cut them into peeces, as if they had been opening of Lambes shut up in their fold. They laid wagers with such as with one thrust of a sword would paunch or bowell a man in the middest, or with one blow of a sword would most readily and most deliverly cut off his head, or that would best pierce his entrals at one stroake.[2]

Bartholomew de las Casas recorded his impressions of the way the Spanish conquistadors treated the native peoples they defeated.

the Spaniards—until an amazing event saved their lives and gave de Soto the trustworthy guide he needed so desperately.

Near sunset, the Spaniards spied a party of about twenty Indians and charged. The Indians turned and fled—all except one. One of the Spaniards rushed toward the Indian and was about to lance him, when the Indian expertly stopped the lance thrust and called out, "Sirs, for the love of God and of St. Mary, do not kill me; I am a Christian, like you, and I am a native of Seville, and my name is Juan Ortiz."[3]

The Spaniards were completely stunned. This person looked just like the Indians. He was deeply tanned. He wore a feather headdress and was tattooed. He carried a bow and arrow. But he was, indeed, Spanish, although he had not spoken a word of Spanish for over ten years.

Juan Ortiz, a youth of eighteen years, had been a member of an earlier Spanish expedition to the coast of Florida led by Panfilo de Narváez in 1528. Ortiz and three others had been captured by local Uzita Indians.

Juan Ortiz, who had survived an early Spanish expedition to America, would become a vital asset to de Soto's mission.

The three other men had been slowly executed. Juan Ortiz faced the same fate, but the wife and three daughters of the chief begged to save the life of the handsome youth. The chief granted their request, and Juan became a family slave. He was forced to gather food, water, and firewood. For several years, Ortiz lived with the Uzita. Later, he escaped. The nearby Mucoco tribe protected him. Ortiz continued to live with the Mucoco without any hope of ever seeing Spain or even another Spaniard again. When de Soto's expedition landed just a few miles away, the chief of the Mucoco sent Ortiz to seek out the Spaniards with an offer of friendship. The Indians met the Spanish on their way to de Soto's camp.[4]

Juan Ortiz became de Soto's trusted translator. Ortiz talked with de Soto and informed him of a large agricultural Indian tribe, the Ocale, who lived inland to the north. They would have supplies of corn that de Soto could take. There were also rumors of gold to be found in the Ocale territory. With these exciting prospects, de Soto soon moved his expedition inland in search of gold and glory.

Chapter 2

The Indians of North America

The first people to live in North America were hunters, who arrived between twenty-five thousand and forty thousand years ago. They came into present-day Alaska from the Asian mainland across the Bering Strait land bridge near the North Pole, following the paths of the animals they hunted.

They adapted quickly to being the first humans in a bountiful and beautiful land. They quickly spread southward and eastward. Eventually, people spread across all of North America. There were nomadic hunters and gatherers living in Florida ten thousand to twelve thousand years ago. They lived in small groups, with probably no more than fifty people or several related families in each band.[1] The climate was considerably cooler and wetter than it is today.

About eight thousand years ago, the climate started to change, becoming drier and warmer. The forest areas around Texas and northern Mexico were replaced with cactus and other plants that needed little rainfall. The lands of the Midwest became vast prairies of grass. There, few trees survived, except along the rivers that ran from the Rocky Mountains to the Mississippi River that flowed into the Gulf of Mexico. The large animals that had brought the new immigrants to North America gradually disappeared as the climate changed and they were hunted to extinction. East of the Mississippi River, these North American Indians, as these early settlers would later be called, began to hunt the thriving deer, antelope, and other game. They also discovered agriculture and began to set up permanent villages.

The American Southeast

The Southeastern part of what is now the United States was a land covered by trees. From the mangrove trees along the Florida coast to the chestnut and oak hardwood forests in the rolling hills and low mountains in the interior to the north, there were trees everywhere. Clear streams and rivers flowed from the Appalachian mountain highlands through the rolling hills east to the Atlantic Ocean, south to the Caribbean Sea, or west to the Mississippi River.

The rolling hills that make up most of present-day Tennessee, northern Mississippi, Alabama, and Georgia were covered by a vast hardwood forest of chestnut trees, six feet or more in diameter. They towered over the other kinds of hardwoods, such as oak and hickory. These trees provided both animals and humans all kinds of nuts and berries to eat.

South and east of the rolling hills, flatlands called the coastal plain extended to the seashore. The coastal plain makes up most of what is now called the Deep South—the areas of southern Mississippi, Alabama, Georgia, South Carolina, and northern Florida. This area was covered by a dense pine forest. Pine forests, which bear no nuts or berries, offer wildlife little food. Pine needles also cover the ground and prevent other plants from growing. Although the valleys of the rivers that ran through the region supported large settlements of Indians, the areas between the rivers—where the pine forests dominated—were less populated with either animals or people.

The rivers and streams that ran through these forests were teeming with fish, turtles, wild birds, oysters that held freshwater pearls, otters, and beavers. The rivers carried millions of tons of mineral-rich sediment from the mountains and deposited it along the river bends on their way to the sea. Every spring, these rivers would overflow their banks, flood the land, and deposit new layers of rich soil. In the uplands, these rich river bottoms were often covered with vast cane forests much taller than a man on horseback. River cane is a grasslike plant. It grows very quickly, and the local Indians used it for arrows, walls, mats, and the roofs of their homes.[2] The cane forests also made a natural hiding place for white-tailed deer, bears, panthers, turkeys, and even humans.

The Adena Culture

Centered in the Ohio River valley near what is now Chillicothe, Ohio, a large Woodland Indian culture arose around 1000 B.C. It extended its influence along the Ohio River north into Pennsylvania and even as far as New York. It was called the Adena culture.

The Adena people hunted, fished, and gathered food. They lived together in small groups. They constructed circular houses that ranged from eighteen to sixty feet in diameter. The walls were made of wood or cane reeds lashed together with flexible plant material. The overhanging roofs were cone-shaped and made from large sections of tree bark.[3]

Travelers were often mystified by giant mounds built along the Natchez Trace. American Indians constructed these mounds for ceremonial purposes.

The Adena people are known for their elaborate mound building and burial ceremonies. The Adena put their honored dead into graves along with a gift such as a favorite smoking pipe. Then they covered the body with a mound of earth. Some of the mounds had trenches dug around them. As other members of the culture died, they were buried within the same mound and more dirt was placed on top to create a higher, larger mound. The highest Adena burial mound is more than seventy feet high. The Adena often built other mounds in the shapes of giant animals and birds to protect their sacred burial sites. The great serpent mound near Cincinnati, Ohio, is a quarter of a mile long, thirty feet wide, and five feet high. It is built in the shape of a great snake uncoiling.

Hopewell Culture

The Adena culture disappeared from Ohio by about A.D. 200, but it continued to exist in outlying regions, such as what is now New York and the Chesapeake Bay. In its place arose another cultural center, Hopewell, just a few miles away along the Scioto River.

The Hopewell were well organized. Their society was led by an elite upper class, a central chief, and his advisors. The people wore fine furs, woven cloth, and animal-skin robes. They decorated their bodies with bracelets, earrings, and necklaces made of copper, pearls, shell, and bone.

The Hopewell were great traders and artists. Hopewell traders, in canoes dug out of large oak trees, traveled up and down the Ohio and Mississippi rivers. They traded for copper with the Indians of Lake Superior, and mica—a transparent sheetlike rock—with the tribes of the eastern Appalachian Mountains. From the tribes along the Mississippi River they obtained seashells, sharkskin, and alligator teeth. From the west, up the Missouri River, they traded for grizzly bear teeth and obsidian—a black, glasslike volcanic rock. The traders returned to their villages with these raw materials. Hopewell artists then made them into cups, pipes, jewelry, and religious objects. These manufactured goods were then traded to the small tribes living throughout the Southeast.

Hopewell burials were sometimes made in geometric mounds that may have indicated special status for the deceased. There were more than ten thousand such mounds in Ohio alone. One mound near Miamisburg, Ohio, was 68 feet high, 852 feet in circumference, and contained more than 300,000 cubic feet of earth.[4] The rich were buried with treasure, signifying their wealth. In one grave were found twelve thousand pearls, thirty-five thousand pearl beads, twenty thousand shell beads, along with nuggets of copper and silver. In another grave, was found a copper ax weighing 28 pounds, a set of copper breastplates, thousands of pearls, and a skull adorned with a copper nose.[5]

Two major changes happened to the Indians of Southeast America during the height of the Hopewell's civilization. Around A.D. 500, the bow and arrow arrived from the Old World to North America. It made hunting much more efficient. It also made warfare among the tribes much deadlier.[6] Then, around A.D. 200, the Hopewell began to grow small-eared tropical flint corn. This early variety of corn needed a hot, dry climate. It was unsuited to the cold and wet weather of the Ohio River valley. It needed a lot of work to plant and grow, but it did help to provide the food surpluses the Hopewell needed to support the traders, artists, and upper classes who did not work at hunting or gathering.[7]

The Cahokia

Between A.D. 800 and 1100, new population centers began to appear all over the Southeast that had been influenced by the Hopewell people. The greatest of these was Cahokia, centered three miles east of present-day St. Louis, Missouri.

There, the Mississippi River created vast flood plains of rich river sediment. Every spring, the Mississippi overflowed its banks and fertilized these vast fields. As a result, the local Indians were able to grow abundant crops of corn, beans, squash, pumpkins, and other staples to support a huge number of people. At its largest, forty thousand people lived within the immediate area of Cahokia. It was the largest city in North America until Philadelphia, Pennsylvania, grew larger in 1800.

Cahokia was ruled by a single chief, called the Great Sun, who lived with his relatives atop a vast earthen mound. The Cahokia constructed their mounds by bringing in huge loads of dirt and stomping it down with their feet. The mounds helped the city avoid the seasonal floods of the nearby river. There were other advantages, too. Breezes were fresher and the view better from the top of the mounds. Great ceremonial importance was given to those who lived atop the mounds, closer to the heavens. The Cahokia would build steps up the sides of the mounds, fifteen to twenty feet wide, by sinking thick logs into the earth as wide as they wanted the steps, and then laying wooden planks on top of these.

During its history, the main mound at Cahokia was rebuilt fourteen times. At its greatest extent, it was over a hundred feet high and had a base a thousand feet long and seven hundred feet wide. This was larger than the pyramids of Egypt. On top of the mound was a home the size of three tennis courts for the great chief. Surrounding the great chief's mound was a large plaza. It held ceremonial courts, playing fields, temples, and smaller mounds that contained the homes of the nobility and other important people. This central area was surrounded by a wall made of large logs placed vertically into the ground. Outside the walls, thousands of small conical homes—belonging to the rest of the Cahokia—dotted the landscape.[8]

Spread of Mississippian Culture

From Cahokia, Mississippian culture spread across the American Southeast from A.D. 1100 to 1350. In some cases, an existing settlement split into two and part of the group moved to a new, previously unsettled location. In other cases, an existing group of hunter-gatherer Indians began to adopt the more settled ways of Mississippi culture in the interest of their own survival. Strong Mississippian chiefdoms, with their many well-fed warriors, demanded payments known as tribute every year from their less powerful neighbors. Many chiefdoms both paid tribute to a larger more powerful culture and received tribute from other nearby chiefdoms that they dominated. In this way, a confederation was created that provided for both a trade and defensive network for all of the chiefdoms involved. In times of war, chiefs could summon companies of soldiers from the surrounding villages, who would be placed under the command of the head chief.

These new Mississippian chiefdoms appeared in the lower Mississippi Valley, along the Arkansas River and northeast Texas. The Natchez chiefdom centered around the Mississippi city of that name today. Farther south, along the Mississippi River, the Plaquemine culture appeared in the delta where the Mississippi River empties into the Gulf of Mexico. The Moundville culture appeared along the Tombigbee and Black Warrior rivers in what is now Alabama. The Hiwassee Island culture appeared in the Tennessee River valley in Tennessee. The Etowah, Chattahoochee-Apalachicola, Ocmulgee, and Oconee rivers in Georgia all became the centers of other Mississippian settlements. In fact, wherever the rivers of the Southeast deposited their rich sediments on their way to the sea, new chiefdoms arose to take advantage of those naturally fertilized fields to develop a thriving agricultural society.

Along the Gulf coast, the abundantly available seafood allowed the Indians to live without farming all year long with little trouble. One area in present-day Florida, where the Indians threw discarded oyster and clam shells, measured seventeen hundred by nineteen hundred feet and was twelve to fifteen feet high. The Gulf Coast Indians from northern Florida to Texas maintained this easy hunting and gathering lifestyle

The American Indians of the Southeast adapted well to their environment, learning to hunt the wild game that lived in the area.

well into the age of European exploration in the late fifteenth and sixteenth centuries. They hunted in the lands of the interior and gathered the hundreds of wild plants around them, but they did not grow their own food. The soil around the coast was not very fertile. It was salty and sandy. Corn and other crops would hardly grow, and the Indians could get by quite well without the labor of farming. However, over time, these Gulf Coast peoples quickly adopted certain features of Mississippian culture that were important to them: They set up warrior societies and a loose confederation of tribute-paying chiefdoms.

The Other Mississippian Chiefdoms

Cahokia, after reaching the height of its influence, quickly declined and then disappeared around A.D. 1350. Perhaps the population simply grew too large for the surrounding lands to support. Whatever the reason, when the Spanish first visited the area, all that was left were the mounds—now overgrown with trees and weeds. None of the Cahokia—or any other—people remained.

Other Mississippian cultural sites also grew, prospered, and then declined throughout the Southeast. Moundville in Alabama and Etowah in Georgia were large population sites that declined and then were deserted. The Indians were not killed. They simply stopped living in the organized chiefdoms. They either moved to the countryside or became a part of a different chiefdom. When the Spanish first explored the region, there were areas where no people at all lived. In 1540, there were no Indians living along the Savannah River in Georgia. The area around the Cahokia site became known to the Spanish as the Vacant Quarter, because there were no people there.

Other Mississippian cultures, however, both continued and thrived. At the time of Hernando de Soto's expedition, there were still some ten to twelve Mississippian chiefdoms that dominated the Southeast. These Indians spoke at least seven different languages, including Muskogean, Iroquoian, Catawban, Caddoan, Algonquian, Tunican, and Timucuan.[9] None of these Mississippian chiefdoms would survive their contact with the Europeans.

The Spanish in America

The Spaniards came to the Americas for several reasons. Christopher Columbus came to discover a new route to the rich trade in the Orient. A few came to convert the natives to Christianity. But almost all of them came for the adventure and the gold. Fray Toribio of Benevento wrote in 1540, "Gold is . . . worshipped by them as a god; for they come without intermission and without thought, across the sea, to toil and danger, in order to get it."[1]

The Thirst for Gold

The first groups of Spanish colonists in the Americas were brought by Christopher Columbus to the island of Hispaniola in the Caribbean Sea. They quickly grew tired of working in the hot tropical climate. They began to enslave the local Indians and forced them to dig for gold.

On his third voyage to the Caribbean Sea in 1498, the settlers on Hispaniola forced Columbus to divide

Source Document

When we stepped ashore we saw fine green trees, streams everywhere and different kinds of fruit. I called to the two captains to jump ashore with the rest, . . . asking them to bear witness that in the presence of them all I was taking possession of this island for their Lord and Lady the King and Queen, and I made the necessary declaration which are set down at greater length in the written testimonies.

Soon many of the islanders gather round us. I could see that they were people who would be more easily converted to our Holy Faith by love than by coercion, and wishing them to look on us with friendship I gave some of them read bonnets and glass beads which they hung round their necks. . . .[2]

Christopher Columbus's voyages to the New World sparked a wave of exploration of the Americas, and led to new opportunities for men like de Soto to win wealth and fame.

the Arawak Indian people among the white settlers to serve as forced laborers. This system was called *repartimiento,* which means "a division" in Spanish. It was later modified in 1503 and called an *encomienda,* which comes from the Spanish verb that means "to entrust."[3] No matter what the system was called, it was

Queen Isabella of Spain sponsored early expeditions to the New World.

slavery and it would be responsible for the deaths of millions of Indians in North and South America over the next hundred years.

In 1502, Nicolas Ovando was appointed governor of the island of Hispaniola. It was his duty to complete the conquest of the island from the remaining Indians on the island. He established fifteen settlements, many of them designed to be gold-mining towns. In each town, the Spanish settlers were awarded the labor of some of the hundreds of thousands of local Indians to work in the gold mines that had been opened. Gold production in Hispaniola peaked before 1517, but even in that year, 118,524 ounces of gold were smelted on the island. The king of Spain, as the sponsor of the gold-mining colony, received one fifth of the total gold produced.

Extremadura

Many of the most distinguished new Spanish settlers and explorers in the New World came from one province. Extremadura was a desolate, mountainous region of Spain that was very poor. The area's major income was obtained through the regular smuggling that went on over the nearby border with Portugal. The rugged land produced rugged men. Many of the most famous conquerors of the newly discovered New World came from Extremadura: Hernándo Cortés, the conqueror of the Aztec Empire of Mexico; Vasco Núñez de Balboa, the discoverer of the Pacific Ocean; Francisco Pizarro, the man who would conquer the Incan Empire of Peru; and many others—including Hernando de Soto.

It was good that the citizens of the region were so hardy. Twice during Hernando de Soto's early boyhood, droughts caused widespread famine in southern Spain. Witnesses described the dead lying in the countryside and refugees walking down the roads carrying their dead children on their backs. During the 1507 famine, an epidemic of bubonic plague struck southern Spain, killing fifteen hundred people in one part of the large city of Seville in just one week in May.

These terrible conditions made the young men of Extremadura very eager to borrow money so they could enlist for the unknown dangers and miseries of life in the New World. No matter what the land across the ocean would bring, the slightest chance for riches, glory, and adventure was much more attractive than a life of poverty and disease at home.[4]

Early Trips to the American Southeast

Everywhere the Spaniards went—Central America, Mexico, and what is now the United States—the first exploring expeditions included some Spaniards who were searching for slaves, in addition to the gold rumored to be so plentiful in the New World. By 1513, there were Spanish settlements on the islands of Cuba, Jamaica, and Puerto Rico. Wherever the Spanish settled, they enslaved the local Indians. The Indians died off quickly as they were overworked in the fields and mines. Spanish slavers then began to explore nearby islands to find more Indians to enslave.

In 1513, Juan Ponce de Leon stopped during a slaving expedition along the Atlantic coast of Florida near present-day Miami. There, he met members of the Tequesta people, who had lived in the area for thousands of years. Ponce de Leon called the land *la Florida.*[5] From Spanish, the term translates as "full of flowers."

In 1514, Pedro de Salazar reached the Atlantic coast of what is today South Carolina on another slaving venture. Salazar thought he had reached the shore of another large island. He managed to capture some Indians who were taller than those who lived on the Caribbean islands. He took them back to

Hispaniola. The myth soon grew that Salazar had discovered a "land of giants."

Salazar confided the location of the "land of giants" to the Spanish governor of Hispaniola who, in 1521, gave the information to the captain of another slaving expedition, Francisco Gordillo. When Gordillo could find no slaves in the Bahamas, he followed Salazar's route to the "land of the giants." About sixty of the local Indians came to investigate the European ship. Gordillo convinced them to come aboard, then he captured them, raised anchor, and sailed back to Hispaniola. The Indians were enslaved and sold to various Spanish masters.

An artist depicted one of the Spaniards' preferred methods of punishing the Indians—cutting off limbs.

31

In 1519, the governor of Jamaica sent Alonso Alvarez de Pineda on a voyage to discover whether these new lands on the Atlantic coast might have a water passage that would allow ships to sail westward through America, all the way to the Orient. Pineda sailed around the Gulf coast from Mexico to Florida. He passed the mouth of a mighty river, which he called the River of Flowers. This was probably the first European notice of the Mississippi River, which soon

The Spanish came to be feared by the native peoples of America because they were known to use their fierce dogs to kill Indians who disobeyed Spanish orders.

became known as the *Rio de la Espiritu Sancto,* or the River of the Holy Spirit.

Pineda's voyage resulted in a map that showed that there was a huge land mass north of the Gulf of Mexico. Now, the question remained: How far north did North America continue, and what rich Indian civilizations were there to be conquered?[6]

Narváez

On December 11, 1526, the king of Spain, Emperor Charles V, signed a new contract naming Panfilo de Narváez captain-general and governor of the unexplored land of Florida. Narváez's expedition of five ships, carrying over six hundred settlers, left Spain on June 17, 1527. They were blown off course during a storm near Cuba and were forced to land on the western coast of Florida. Finally, on June 20, 1528, they entered the lands of the Apalachee Indians near present-day Tallahassee, Florida.

The Apalachee were a fierce tribe of warriors. Narváez made a fatal mistake when he seized one of the tribal chiefs and tried to make him tell the Spaniards if there was any gold nearby. For the month that the expedition stayed in the area, the Spaniards were constantly attacked by the angry Apalachee. Finally, Narváez gave up.

The Spaniards moved to the small town of Aute, closer to the coast. They began to build small boats that would be able to take them around the Gulf of Mexico to the Spanish settlement at Veracruz,

Charles V, the young emperor of Spain and the Holy Roman Empire, was a strong supporter of de Soto's efforts to stake a claim in North America.

Mexico, which was to the west. It took them forty-seven days to build five small boats. In the meantime, they came so close to starving that they began to kill their horses for food. On September 22, 1528, they finally left the land of their Apalachee tormentors and once again faced the dangers of life at sea.

They stayed together until they passed the mouth of a river with an extremely strong current. It was the Mississippi. After that, they encountered some storms and the boats became separated. The men became so exhausted and weak that they could not row any longer. Three of the boats were beached on the Texas coast. The few men who survived were captured and enslaved by local Indians. Narváez's boat was carried into the Gulf of Mexico. He was never seen again.

In October 1534, the four survivors of the six hundred men who had begun the expedition escaped from their Indian masters. They began an amazing adventure, walking across Texas and northern Mexico. On April 1, 1536, Spanish slave hunters near the Pacific coast of northern Mexico found them. One of the men, Alvar Nuñez Cabeza de Vaca, soon returned to Spain, where he wrote a history of the Narváez expedition and his own unbelievable adventures.

The next man to dare to penetrate North America from the south would be one of the greatest of the Spanish conquistadors. He was a man who had arrived in the New World as a thirteen-year-old boy and had risen to become one of the wealthiest men in Spain with a well-deserved reputation as a hero. His name was Hernando de Soto.

De Soto's Early Career

Hernando de Soto was the son of Francisco Méndez de Soto and Leonor Arias Tinoco. He was born in the province of Extremadura, Spain, sometime around the year 1500.

The de Soto family was poor, but had the respect of the other members of the community. Hernando had an older brother, Juan, and two sisters, Catalina and Maria. Hernando could read and write but he probably had no formal education. His early youth was likely spent in swordplay, learning to ride a horse, and listening to or reading romances and adventure stories that were being published by the new invention that was quickly sweeping Europe—the printing press. Also being published at that time were reports of the Spanish colonists in the New World recently discovered by Christopher Columbus.

Hernando de Soto rose from humble beginnings to become one of the best known conquistadors in history.

Panama

Rumors of abundant gold in the land of Panama sent back to Spain by explorer Vasco Núñez de Balboa result-ed in a massive rush to settle the area. Spanish King Ferdinand financed the expedition, appointing Pedrarias Dávila to be governor of the new lands.

In the late summer of 1513, more than fifteen hun-dred people lined up in Seville, Spain, to join the expedition. Among others from Extremadura, thirteen-year-old Hernando de Soto and his friend Hernán Ponce de Leon borrowed enough money from a banker to buy the swords and equipment they needed to apply for positions as foot soldiers.[1] The massive expedition of twenty-one ships sailed from Spain on April 11, 1514, arriving in Panama on June 26.

From the beginning, the new colony in Panama faced disaster. There were simply too many people and not enough food. Dávila had ordered that as soon as the new settlers reached land, they could no longer use food or supplies from the ships. They were expected to get their food and support from the local Indians.

The small town where they landed, Santa Maria de Antiqua de Darien, was a small village of about a hundred native-style huts built by the few Spaniards already living in the town. There had been a recent plague of locusts, and there was little extra food available to feed all the new arrivals. Many starved.

To make matters worse, almost immediately upon their arrival, the new settlers came down with an unidentified epidemic they called the *modorra,* or "the lethargy." More than seven hundred people died or fled back to the more settled islands of the Caribbean.[2] De Soto, however, remained and toughed it out in Panama.

Nata

Between 1514 and 1519, Dávila ordered the Spanish settlers to go on raids, scouring the countryside for food, slaves, and, as always, gold. Hernando de Soto's fame began on August 1, 1520, during one such expedition to the northwest coast of Panama. The raid was led by Gaspar de Espinosa, who divided his forces into two parts. He himself commanded the first group of explorers, which traveled north by ship from the Pacific coast port of Panama. The rest of the men, including de Soto, were put under the command of Francisco Pizarro. They marched overland and planned to meet Espinosa's group near the Indian village of Nata.

Pizarro put de Soto, now around twenty years old, in command of a squad of thirty men who were to march at the front of the expedition. It was an uneventful trip until they had come quite close to their agreed-on meeting place.

As they approached Nata, de Soto's men heard the sounds of a battle being fought ahead. De Soto spurred his men ahead and soon came to an overlook. There, he saw Urraca Indians attacking Espinosa's men, who were trapped in a gully in the valley below.

De Soto charged. He led his men down into the valley and attacked the Indians, who outnumbered his forces thirty to one. This brave move caught the Indians totally by surprise. They halted their attack on Espinosa giving his men a chance to retreat to safety.

Espinosa then moved into the town of Nata and set up a home base from which to lead other raids into the countryside. He left de Soto and fifty other men under the command of Francisco Compañón to guard the garrison. As soon as Espinosa led the main body of the expedition away, the Indians attacked and quickly surrounded the few Spaniards, who hid behind their makeshift defenses.

Hernando de Soto and Pedro Miguel led a small party of horsemen through the enemy lines and rode one hundred miles to Panama in just two days to alert Dávila. Dávila sent a ship under the command of de Soto's friend Hernán Ponce de León with forty men to stop the Indian siege of Nata. Dávila then led another party of 140 men overland as additional support. All of the reinforcements arrived in time to fight a battle that lasted five days. The Spanish killed many of the Indians before they could withdraw into the countryside. After the battle, Dávila remained a short time in Nata and divided the lands and captured Indians among the victorious Spaniards.

For the next four years, between August 1519 and late 1523, Hernando de Soto lived a fine life in this fertile valley, amassing whatever gold and Indian slaves he could get.[3] By this time, he was no longer an inexperienced youth. He was a rich, seasoned veteran of numerous Indian campaigns. He was also well respected among his fellow Spaniards as a brave and crafty leader of men.

Nicaragua

Despite Dávila and de Soto's success, the lands north of Nata remained unconquered. To change that, many prominent conquistadors wanted to lead an expedition into the land called Nicaragua. In 1522, Gil González Dávila took a small expedition in ships his men had built themselves on the Pacific Coast near Panama and explored the Pacific Coast as far north as the Gulf of Fonseca, near what is now Honduras.

Eager to retain control over the region, in the fall of 1523 the governor of Panama, Pedrarias Dávila, appointed Francisco Hernández de Córdoba to lead a hastily put-together expedition of over two hundred men to try to conquer Nicaragua, too.[4] De Soto signed on with the Córdoba expedition to be the commander of one of its three marching companies. He would lead seventy-six men.

The expedition left Panama in late 1523 and spent the year 1524 fighting the native Indian tribes in western Nicaragua. Córdoba's forces founded the Spanish towns of Granada, León, and Segovia. In León, de Soto was named a minor town official. He built a house on the same square as the town's church. He owned many Indians as slaves, and he used them to work both his estates in the area and his gold mines in the mountains. By 1533, de Soto was one of the six richest men in Central America.

The Empire of Peru

For years, de Soto's old friend and captain from the expeditions in Panama, Francisco Pizarro, had been trying to reach what was supposed to be the seat of a vast empire in the mountains of South America. Most of the jewelry and other articles of gold that the Spanish found in Panama had come from the lands to the south. There were rumors of great quantities of gold to be found in a land called Peru. In 1530, Pizarro had sailed back to Spain and received a formal contract from the Crown to conquer Peru. With that contract, Pizarro could offer recruits a percentage of whatever gold and treasure they might find, which would appeal to experienced men.

Pizarro sent some of his men all over the Spanish provinces in the New World looking for recruits to be part of his mission. Of course, Pizarro's men specifically sought out Hernando de Soto. He was known as a fearless decision-maker in the wild countryside, and a

Source Document

This Garden was in the Incas time a Garden of Silver and Gold, as they had in the Kings houses, where they had many sorts of Hearbes, Flowers, Plants, Trees, Beasts great and small, wilde, tame, Snakes, Lizards, Snailes, Butterflies, small and great Birds, each set in their place. . . . They had also in the house heapes of wood, all counterfeit of Gold and Silver, as they had in the house royall: likewise they had great statues of men and women, and children. . . . Like to this Temple of Cozco were others in many Provinces of that Kingdome, in which every Curaca indevoured according to his power to have such riches of Gold and Silver.[5]

Hernando de Soto was among the conquistadors who defeated the great Incan Empire of Peru. The incredible wealth of the Inca people inspired one Spanish writer to record this description.

man who excelled at leading troops against hostile Indians. He was a shrewd player in the life-and-death struggle of conquistador politics. He was also rich, and he owned a ship that could be used to transport supplies to Peru. For being part of the expedition, de Soto was made a captain of cavalry, one of the top leaders of the expedition. He received a large share of the jewels and gold taken from the wealthy Inca civilization. He was also promised that he would be appointed governor of the richest city the Spaniards conquered.

The Conquest of Peru

In January 1531, the *San Geronimo*—with Hernando de Soto in command—and two other ships left port in Panama, heading south toward Peru. They were about to become much richer.

In Peru, it would be de Soto who rode his horse at a gallop right at the Incan Emperor Atahualpa, sliding to a stop just inches from the seated commander of tens of thousands of gathered troops, who was taken prisoner. It was de Soto who had received the third largest share of the more than twenty thousand pounds of gold and silver ransom Atahualpa put into two large rooms to win his freedom. When the treasure was later melted down, it was valued at 1.326 million pesos (Spanish currency) of gold and 51,610 marks (also a currency) of silver—worth today nearly $100 million.

Presentation at Court

After his years in Peru, in the spring of 1536, de Soto returned to Spain. Back home, de Soto met formally with Emperor Charles V. The young emperor was the same age as de Soto. He had inherited not only the kingdom of Spain but also the vast Holy Roman Empire, which included huge territories of what is now Germany, the Netherlands, and parts of France and Italy.

De Soto (on horseback) helped defeat the Incan Empire, by taking Emperor Atahualpa prisoner.

Charles was happy to see de Soto. The emperor granted de Soto membership in the Order of Santiago, a high honor. He also gave de Soto a new mission.

Charles wanted to control North America, the vast, unknown land that stretched from Mexico to the Atlantic Ocean, and farther north. He needed to ensure the safe passage of his ships, carrying Aztec and Incan gold and silver, from any pirates who might lay in wait along the way back to Spain. Controlling North America would help with this goal.

North America was still mysterious. It was still a land surrounded by myths, such as the fountain of youth, a legendary spring that would make people immortal. It was a risk, however. No one so far had even survived, much less found any cities of gold. Charles believed it would take someone with de Soto's many talents to conquer America successfully.

On April 20, 1537, Charles V signed the *capitulacion*—the contract that spelled out de Soto's duties and rewards for the exploration of North America. De Soto's contract gave him the exclusive right for four years to conquer, pacify, and populate the lands from the Rio de las Palmas north of Veracruz in central Mexico, across the Caribbean Sea to the tip of Florida, and up the Atlantic coast of North America to north of Chesapeake Bay. He was to lead an army of at least five hundred soldiers and provide them with all of the supplies needed for an eighteen-month trip.

He was then directed to choose about five hundred miles of coastal land in the North American territory to set up a province. De Soto was named the governor of that province for the rest of his life. As governor, he would be granted the official title of respect, *adelantado,* which means "one who pushes forward." Not only would he govern this land as well as the island of Cuba, but he would also be the *alguazil mayor,* or the highest judge, of the local courts. He was also given the title to twenty-five square miles of land anywhere in the province, so he could maintain a private residence.

De Soto was to pay all the expenses for the entire expedition. De Soto was also given the duty of taking along members of the religious orders to convert the Indians to Christianity. In addition to all of these requirements, the emperor warned that if de Soto failed to fulfill any of his obligations, "we will order that you be punished, and proceed against you as against one who keeps not nor complies with, but acts counter to, the commands of his natural king and lord."[6] Several representatives of the emperor were assigned to go along to make sure that all of the terms of the contract were carried out.

A few days later, Emperor Charles V called a meeting of the Order of Santiago at his palace. Hernando de Soto, dressed in his most spectacular suit of armor, knelt before the assembled members and was presented with a brilliant white tunic embroidered with the red crosses of the Order. He was now a member of the most important military brotherhood in the country.

As he left the palace, he climbed into a coach decorated with his family coat of arms—a golden eagle on a field of blood red. The man who had been born to a poor family in Extremadura was now ready to conquer a new world.

Chapter 5

The Expedition Begins

After his interview with Emperor Charles V in April 1537, de Soto went to Seville and began the stupendously detailed work of outfitting a large expedition to the unexplored wilds of North America.

One of the men de Soto met in Seville when he returned was Juan de Añasco, a man of many talents. Añasco was a sailor, mapmaker, navigator, and astrologer. He was a recognized leader and organizer. De Soto decided to make him the *contador,* or accountant, for the new expedition. It was an important job that included making lists of the items needed, as well as finding those items, paying for them, and ensuring that they were delivered and preserved for the voyage.

On September 3, 1537, de Soto bought *La Magdalena,* a large ship of eight hundred tons. Two days later, he bought the *San Juan.* By the time he was ready to sail, he had bought another five large ships and several smaller ones. With help from Añasco, de Soto contracted with bakers to produce and deliver forty tons of hardtack—hard biscuits that did not spoil easily that were to be eaten aboard ship. He also bought huge quantities of wine and olive oil, as well as salt-cured meat in hundreds of wooden casks. In addition, he bought hundreds of empty wooden casks to be filled with fresh water just before the expedition left Spain.

Besides food and drink, de Soto bought shovels, collars to hold enslaved Indians, chain link for armor, swords, crossbows, and guns. He also bought gunpowder, and leather to make boots, belts, and harnesses. He bought beads, mirrors, and other goods to trade with the natives.

All the supplies were very expensive. Together, they cost more than six times what the Spanish king had spent on the Dávila expedition that had brought de Soto to Panama twenty years before. Amazingly, de Soto paid for everything himself.

Cabeza de Vaca

On August 9, 1537, Alvar Nuñez Cabeza de Vaca, one of the four survivors of the Narváez expedition to North America, returned to Spain and had a private meeting with the emperor. Cabeza de Vaca delivered not only a report of the fate of the others in the expedition, but also told of the riches of the American Southeast and the wonders that he had seen there. Cabeza de Vaca's return caused a sensation in Spain. His insistence on a private talk with the emperor sparked rumors that the lands of North America were indeed filled with fantastic treasures.

De Soto later spoke directly with Cabeza de Vaca about returning with him as a lieutenant on the new expedition. Cabeza de Vaca refused. He did not want to be second-in-command to anyone ever again. When others asked Cabeza de Vaca whether they should go along with de Soto, however, he enthusiastically advised them to sell their possessions and go.

Baltasar de Gallegos, one of Cabeza de Vaca's relatives, sold his houses and vineyards to raise the money to go. He spent four thousand gold ounces to equip himself with the armor, clothes, weapons, horses, slaves, and servants he took along on the expedition. De Soto made Gallegos chief constable, and overtime, came to rely on him.

Men of the Expedition

De Soto sent Luis de Moscoso and Juan Ruiz Lobillo to tour the country and sign up recruits for the expedition. It was not hard to find capable men who were eager to go. The men who signed on were not members of the Spanish Army. They had no formal military training. Instead, they were civilians, who had to present proof that they were good, law-abiding people.

Some of those who enlisted with de Soto were noblemen, but certainly not all. They came from a variety of backgrounds. Some were craftsmen, merchants, and clergymen. At least five were freed black slaves. Many of the men were related to each other, and some were related to de Soto. Most members of the expedition were neighbors.

Approximately seven hundred men signed up for the expedition between January 29 and March 15, 1538. More than 40 percent of them came from the fifty-six towns of de Soto's home province, Extremadura. Over thirty others came from nearby towns over the border in Portugal. Most of the others came from the Spanish provinces of Castile and Aragon.

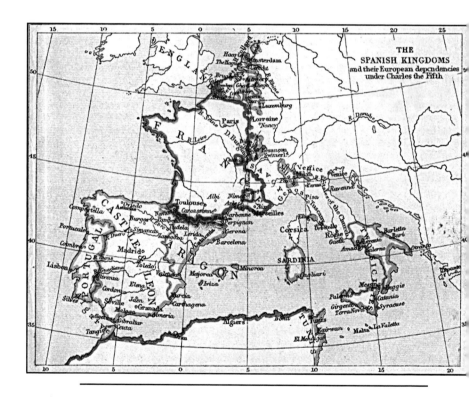

Some of the men on Hernando de Soto's expedition came from Portugal and the Spanish provinces of Castile and Aragon.

The men of the expedition were young, with an average age of about twenty-four. Almost all of them could sign their name—but that does not mean they could read. Not many people of the time could. Usually, everyone who enlisted in an expedition was required to provide his own weapons and supplies. It had been that way back when young de Soto borrowed money to go to Panama. However, it was not so for his expedition. De Soto invested much of his own fortune to pay many of the expedition's expenses.

The expedition also hired blacksmiths; farriers to shoe horses; carpenters; a surgeon; a druggist; a navigator; ships' captains; and sailors. By the time de Soto left, he had hired over 130 sailors who would never actually step foot in North America. They would remain with the fleet, ready to bring reinforcements as they were needed.

De Soto selected the three agents of the king who would accompany the expedition: the accountant, the royal witness, and the treasurer, who would guard the king's share of any gold or other treasure that was found. In addition, de Soto was required to pay the expenses of the priests who were to go on the expedition to try to convert the Indians.

Women of the Expedition

In addition to the many men, there were twelve women who went with the de Soto expedition when it left Spain. Almost all of these ladies were married to members of the expedition, and their passage had been paid by their husbands. Most of these ladies established homes on the island of Cuba when the rest of the expedition sailed for Florida. Isabel de Bobadilla, Hernando de Soto's wife, remained in Cuba. A niece of de Soto's, who was married to expedition member Carlos Enriquez, also traveled to Cuba. Maria de Guzman, the wife of de Soto's constable, Baltasar de Gallegos, set up a home in Cuba, too.

Six other women also registered to go: Isabel de Herrera and her daughter, Inés de Herrera; Leonor de Volaños and her daughter, Isabel de Mejía; Inés Rodriguez; and Isabel Sayaga. Historians are not sure who these women were, but it is likely they were the wives or girlfriends of expedition members who hoped to begin a new life in the New World.

The Expedition Departs

On April 1, 1538, de Soto held the first inspection of the new recruits. Most of the men showed up in their finest suits, colorful silks, and stylish hats with feathered plumes. De Soto told them all to go home and return the next day in their armor. The next day, he was just as displeased. Most of them showed up in rusted or broken suits of armor. He quickly dismissed the worst of these. The rest of the men quickly packed their belongings for the long journey and said their good-byes.

The expedition sailed from the harbor of San Lúcar on April 7, 1538, for Santiago, Cuba, with approximately six hundred fifty to seven hundred people. De Soto, the commander of the fleet, sailed aboard the *San Cristóbal,* a new ship that had been constructed for the expedition. On Easter Sunday, the expedition stopped at the Canary Islands off the northwestern coast of Africa to fill its water casks and buy fresh supplies. De Soto and his wife, Isabel, called on the governor of the island, a relative of hers, and persuaded him to allow his teenage daughter, Leonor de Bobadilla, to accompany them as Isabel's companion. Leonor would later stay with Isabel at the de Soto home in Cuba while Hernando de Soto traveled on to North America.

The expedition arrived at Santiago, a small town on the southern coast of Cuba, in June 1538. De Soto landed his men and assigned them to live in the homes of the people of the area. He paid for their food, but the local residents complained about his high-handed manner. As the new governor, however, he could do pretty much whatever he wanted on the island, and for the next eleven months, he concentrated on getting his expedition ready to head to the American Southeast.

Preparations for the Journey

As part of his preparation, de Soto bought almost all the cattle and horses he could find. The de Soto expedition arrived in Florida with about 225 horses.[1] The horses used by the Spaniards were originally bred on the Barbary Coast of North Africa. They were first brought into Spain by the Moors, or North Africans, who had invaded Spain in the eighth century. They were small horses with hard bones and strong tendons. They could carry heavy loads for long distances at fast speeds. They could work on little food, and would continue to work even after being seriously wounded.

The Indians of America were amazed by the horses. At the time, there were no horses in North America. They had been extinct for millions of years. At first sight, the Indians thought horse and rider were one animal—a fantastic creature of speed and death they had never even imagined before. The Spaniards increased the terrifying effect by putting many small copper bells on their saddles and bridles to create a sound that would frighten the Indians.

Later, the Indians came to believe that the horses were immortal. The Spaniards took care to bury dead horses secretly at night to keep up this illusion. Even after the Indians found out the truth about horses, they still respected the animal's power and avoided them as much as possible. Spanish riders could use long lances or their swords very effectively from their high saddles. Both the Spaniards and the Indians felt that horses were more valuable than men. The Spaniards often risked the lives of infantrymen to guard their horses instead. When a horse was killed, the Indians rejoiced much more than when they killed three or four Spaniards.[2]

In Cuba, de Soto bought several farms where he could grow the fresh food he would need to feed his crew. He also bought most of the available manufactured goods, and even started to recruit additional men from the island.

De Soto sent the women and most of the men by sea from Santiago to Havana, on the north side of Cuba. Then, he took about one hundred fifty of the cavalry, mounted on their new horses, and made a slow training march across the island. They reached Havana at the end of March 1539.

There, de Soto sent Juan de Añasco and the other navigators in a small boat to locate Tampa Bay, the site of their proposed landing in Florida. During their trip, they captured several Indians, who would serve the expedition as guides and interpreters.

De Soto appointed his wife, Isabel, to be the governor of Cuba while he was gone. On May 10, 1539, he made out his will. In it, he instructed that he should be buried in a new chapel to be built with his money in the church of San Miguel at home in Jerez de los Caballeros. He also wanted the red cross of the Order of Santiago displayed on its altar. He directed that money be set aside to have a priest say prayers in his memory at the altar every day.

Finally, all the members of the expedition were loaded aboard nine ships. On May 18, 1539, they left Havana harbor to fulfill de Soto's mission of discovery and conquest for the emperor of Spain.[3]

The Expedition to Mabila

Usually, de Soto's expedition moved in three companies: a vanguard (advance group), the main body of the expedition, and a rear guard. The vanguard was composed of horsemen and sometimes a few foot soldiers. They led the way and cleared the path for the others to follow. De Soto usually traveled with this group. Behind them came the main body of the expedition. It consisted of a few horsemen as guards, most of the foot soldiers, the Indian porters who carried the supplies, and the servants and ladies. De Soto had brought a large herd of pigs, which was to be used as emergency rations. It traveled with the main body, controlled by several men on horses. He had also brought several large packs of dogs trained to hunt and kill Indians. These, too, traveled with the main body of the expedition. They were handled on leashes by trained Spanish foot soldiers. Behind the main body of the expedition came a small rear guard of horsemen, whose role was to protect the main body from attack.

As de Soto started north from present-day Tampa Bay, he began a trip through the vast southeastern American pine forest that extended north for hundreds of miles.[1] As the expedition traveled, it encountered many animals that are now extinct: the giant ivory-billed woodpecker, passenger pigeons, the green and yellow Carolina parakeet, and certain types of panthers, bears, and wolves. The travelers also saw millions upon millions of longleaf, loblolly, and slash pine trees.

De Soto's conquistadors moved north constantly, searching for fields of corn, American Indians, and any sign of the gold they hoped to find. They reached the Withlacoochee River and the Great Ocale Swamp.

The Great Ocale Swamp

The swamp was a low wetlands about twenty-five miles long and six miles wide that ran along the main channel of the river. Huge cypress trees sheltered the shorter oak, cedar, palmetto, and cabbage palm trees that grew beneath them. On the swamp floor grew several types of evergreen shrubs, such as yaupon holly and wax myrtle. There were vines everywhere, thorny bamboo, and poison ivy—which delayed any forward movement by the expedition. The swamp was also filled with wild turkey, herons, wood storks, and ibis.

The area was very beautiful, but also very dangerous. As the expedition crossed the swamp, Indians

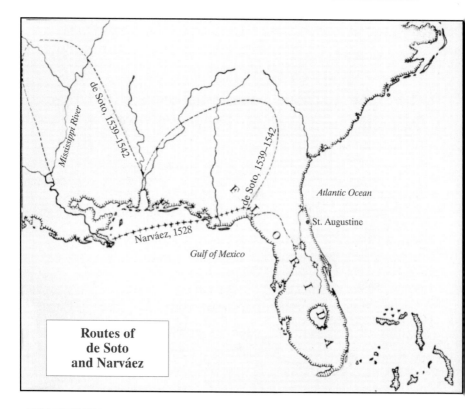

This map shows the routes taken by de Soto and Narváez through the American Southeast.

would suddenly appear, fire their arrows, and sink back into the thick underbrush before the Spaniards could even react. Even worse, several horses drowned before the expedition successfully crossed the Withlacoochee River and came to the fertile fields of the Ocale Indians.

When de Soto and his vanguard entered the lands of the Ocale Indians on July 26, 1537, the outlying villages were deserted. Finding a little corn, they sent some of it back for those who were still coming through the Ocale Swamp, and ate all the rest of it quickly.

De Soto sent one of the few Indians they had captured along the march into the countryside to ask the local chief to meet with the Spaniards. The chief, who had a twenty-year history of carefully avoiding Spanish slaving expeditions, sent back a refusal. He said, "I already know very well what your customs and behavior are like. To me you are professional vagabonds who wander from place to place, gaining your livelihood by robbing, sacking, and murdering people who have given you no offense." The chief went on,

> I promise to maintain war upon you so long as you wish to remain in my province, not by fighting in the open, although I could do so, but by ambushing and waylaying you whenever you are off guard . . . I shall be content to behead only two of you each week since I thus can slay all of you within a few years.[2]

The Indians did succeed in killing a few of the Spaniards, beheading them as the chief promised. After the Spaniards buried the bodies, the Indians came back during the night, dug up the bodies, cut them into pieces, and hung them in the trees for the birds to eat. The Indians moved so silently and were so good at hiding that the Spaniards could find only a few of them. These were either killed or enslaved.

De Soto and his men did not stay long in the dangerous province of Ocale. They went first to Acuera, another village to the east. There, they were attacked twice by Indians, and lost three soldiers and a horse.

Once, de Soto and his men were resting after a battle with the Indians. One of the Indians they had captured rose from where he was sitting and with a mighty roar, struck de Soto in the face. Although the other Spaniards quickly killed the Indian, de Soto was unconscious for

Hernando de Soto, wearing his armor, is depicted as he meets with a local chief.

more than half an hour, bleeding from the eyes, nose, and mouth. De Soto survived but lost several teeth.

The expedition soon collected all of the food it could find—enough to last it three months. Then, it quickly moved on.[3]

The Chiefdom of the Apalachee

De Soto left Ocale with fifty horsemen and a hundred foot soldiers on August 11. He went in search of the chiefdom of Apalachee, a kingdom that, according to rumor, was completely surrounded by water. It was the chiefdom that had beaten the Panfilo de Narváez expedition into submission during the first Spanish attempt to colonize the Southeast. De Soto must have heard the terrible story from Cabeza de Vaca while they were in Spain. Even the Indians of Ocale seemed to be deathly afraid of the Apalachee.

De Soto reached the border of Apalachee territory on August 16. He sent eight men back to the main body to bring on the rest of the expedition. These reinforcements arrived on September 4.

The word *Apalachee* means "the land between the rivers." It was a chiefdom about forty miles square around present-day Tallahassee, Florida, located between the Aucilla River to the east, the Ochlockonee River to the north and west, and the Gulf of Mexico to the south. It was indeed a kingdom surrounded by water, with large swamps along the riverbanks.

The Spaniards hacked their way through the swamp, under constant Indian arrow fire. The horses

The Indians had the military advantage over the Spaniards when it came to fighting on the water.

could not be used because of the dense underbrush that filled the swamp. Once the Spaniards had made their way into the open countryside, however, the Indians retreated back into the swamp. They knew they were no match for the mounted cavalry, who could ride them down and kill them with lances.

De Soto entered Anhayca, the large capital city located in present-day Tallahassee, Florida. The town, big enough to house all of the members of the expedition, was completely deserted. The houses were constructed around a central square. De Soto took over the main chief's house.

An Abundant Land

Although the Indians continued constant warfare against the Spaniards from their hiding places in the swamp during the entire time the expedition was in the land of the Apalachee, de Soto was able to feed his crew for five months without looking any farther than five miles in any direction for food. There were fish and shellfish from the sea; meat from the plentiful deer and turkeys; fish and turtles from local lakes; and an abundance of corn. The Indians had also stored pumpkins, beans, and other wild food in both Apalachee and the surrounding smaller villages. Fruit

The Spaniards fought off attacks by Indians throughout the course of their expedition.

and nuts from local trees—acorns, hickory nuts, red mulberry, wild plums, black cherries—blueberries and blackberries, and many edible roots and native plants could also be gathered from the wild. The members of the expedition used the bark and wood of the sassafras tree for teas, medicines, and drinks. It was a bountiful land, and de Soto decided to spend the winter there.

During his stay in Apalachee, de Soto interviewed an Indian boy named Pedro, who had been raised by native traders and had traveled widely. De Soto learned that there was a chiefdom near the Atlantic Ocean to the northeast called Cofitachequi. It had gold, silver, and large quantities of pearls. An expedition to the area during the 1520s had reported the same stories of a nearby land full of riches and pearls. De Soto believed the rumors and decided to move his expedition inland in search of the treasure. He planned to march northeast to find the treasure in the spring and then return to the land of the Apalachee, where food was so easy to obtain, the next fall.

De Soto sent one of his trusted lieutenants, Francisco Maldonado, along the coast to find a suitable port for the ships near the land of the Apalachee that could be used to land reinforcements from Cuba. Two months later, Maldonado returned to report an anchorage, probably Pensacola Bay, that would serve well. It was a large bay with room for many ships to anchor, safe from storms. There was an Indian village nearby called Ochuse whose men could be used as porters and servants.

On February 26, 1540, de Soto sent Maldonado back to Havana, Cuba, with a report for de Soto's wife about what had happened so far. Maldonado was to fill the ship with more food and supplies, including more crossbows, guns, lead, gunpowder, and shoes. He was then to return to Ochuse and wait for de Soto and his men, who would march overland to join Maldonado by the late summer or fall. If they did not show up, Maldonado was supposed to sail along the coast of the Gulf of Mexico to the west as far as the Rio del Espiritu Santo—the Mississippi River—to look for them.

Onward to the Land of Pearls

On March 3, 1540, de Soto left Apalachee in search of the land of treasure Pedro had described. Pedro would accompany the expedition as a guide and interpreter. The men carried with them enough food to feed the expedition for about ten days.

They moved into what is today southwestern Georgia and reached the Indian town of Capachequi. These Indians received the expedition in peace, gave the men food, and allowed them to rest. The expedition left on March 17 after staying there six days.

The Indian towns the expedition visited on its march through present-day Georgia were often surrounded by tall defensive walls of tree trunks planted vertically in the ground. Many also had ceremonial mounds in the center of the village, on which the local chief lived with his family. The local Indians practiced intense corn agriculture on the flood plains of the rivers. They stored their surplus in sheds built near their homes.

The expedition moved on to the Indian village of Ichisi. There, the women of the town met the expedition with plates of hot corn tortillas and wild onions to eat. De Soto brought along many of the friendly Indians of these villages as porters and other servants. Because there were no food supplies, the expedition was forced to be almost constantly on the move. It quickly devoured all of the food resources of the Indian villages and was then forced to move on. Many times, the expedition left a small village with no food reserves to carry the Indians through the winter.

The Ichisi tribe, who lived on the banks of the Ocmulgee River, was genuinely friendly to de Soto. He rested his men at their village for a week. He left on April 2, 1540, traveling to the northeast toward the town of Ocute, the main village of another Mississippian chiefdom.

De Soto arrived on April 9 and was immediately faced with a risky gamble. Even though de Soto's Indian guide and interpreter Pedro told him that the land of pearls was only four days away, the local Indians told him that the lands he sought were more than two weeks away across the uninhabited pine forests on both sides of the Savannah River. They told him there were no Indians and no animals in the barren open lands of the pine forest ahead. If they were right, it would mean starvation for de Soto's expedition if he tried to push on. De Soto demanded that four hundred of the local

Indians accompany him as porters. They would carry whatever food de Soto could carry with him. He then moved on to the town of Cofaqui, the last stop before venturing into the wilderness.

Wilderness of Ocute

The expedition left Cofaqui on April 13, 1540. It traveled nine days without seeing anyone or finding anything to eat. The men would have gladly thrown Pedro to the dogs for lying to them. However, he was still a valuable interpreter. They pushed on from early morning to dusk. It rained almost all the time.

On April 17, the expedition came to the Savannah River. It crossed it where there were several islands in the river. On April 19, it crossed the Salada River. On April 21, the expedition came to yet another river, the Broad, which it crossed at a low-water point. The men were now just a few miles away from present-day Columbia, South Carolina, and they were starving.

Death loomed large. De Soto allowed his Indian porters to return to their lands. He could no longer feed them, and the food they had been carrying was gone. He ordered that some of the pigs that were kept as emergency rations be slaughtered and roasted. Each man was given a pound of meat and some wild greens from the forest. It was delicious, but the men knew they had to find more food quickly or die.

De Soto sent out scouting parties with ten days' rations to look for food. On April 25, Juan de Añasco rode into camp with news that the scouts had discovered a town a day or so's march away that had enough food to save the expedition.

The men reached the small town of Hymahi the very next day and gorged themselves on the stored corn and fresh mulberries and strawberries they found nearby.

Cofitachequi, the Land of Pearls

When the chief of the village of Cofitachequi, located on the Wateree River in present-day central South Carolina, learned that the Spaniards were coming, he ran into the woods to hide. He left his niece to confront the Spanish invaders.

When de Soto reached the banks of the Wateree River on May 1, the young princess crossed the river in a large canoe with eight of her ladies-in-waiting. Her canoe was covered with a large canopy to protect the young women from the sun. The princess's canoe was towed by another large canoe that held many paddlers and warriors. The young princess wore clothes of spun mulberry bark and three large strings of pearls the size of hazelnuts. De Soto was completely charmed by her. He called her the "Lady of Cofitachequi."

She and de Soto sat in the shade and talked for a while. De Soto spoke Spanish to Juan Ortiz, who spoke one Indian dialect to Pedro, who translated into the language of the princess. At the end of their meeting, she gave de Soto the pearls she was wearing.

The Spaniards later found about two hundred pounds of pearls in graves in the central temple mound of the town. De Soto handed them out by the

Cofitachequi shows de Soto her vast supply of pearls and other valuable stones.

handful to his men.[4] However, they found no gold and silver. De Soto then sent Baltasar de Gallegos and a large part of the expedition to a nearby town for more food, which the young princess had offered to give them. Then the expedition moved on.

Through the Land of the Cherokee

On May 13, 1540, de Soto and his men left Cofitachequi and turned northwest into present-day North Carolina. Their goal was to try to locate a source of gold.

De Soto led the expedition through the chiefdoms of the Chalaque people, now known as the Cherokee, located near present-day Charlotte, North Carolina. The Chalaque built round houses. They had little corn, but plenty of turkeys, deer, and little dogs that they raised to eat. However, there were no large reserves of food in these villages and the expedition hastily moved on.

De Soto's men moved out of the pine forests and up into the low Appalachian Mountain forests of mighty chestnut trees up to twelve feet in diameter. They passed the highest streams of the North Toe River near present-day Spruce Pine, North Carolina, and continued westward. They followed the river, crossing it many times, and finally reached the point where it joins the Nolichucky River near present-day Embreeville, Tennessee. There, they met some Indians from the peaceful chiefdom of Guasili.

On May 31, the expedition moved down the Nolichucky River to the chiefdom of Chiaha, arriving on June 5. De Soto had left the land of the Cherokee.

The Chiefdom of Chiaha

Chiaha was a large agricultural town with plenty of corn for the hungry men of the expedition. It was built on an island in the French Broad River near present-day Dandridge, Tennessee. De Soto, worn out by the rugged terrain of the mountains, rested for almost a month in Chiaha.

The Indians of this town were the northernmost ally of the great chiefdom of Coosa to the south. Chiaha was a land of plenty, and the late spring climate was pleasant. The Spaniards found pearls from the mussels in the river. They played and swam with the local Indians, and they rested and repaired their equipment. They grew healthy on a diet of bear fat, honey, and fresh fruit.

From Chiaha, de Soto sent two men on to Chisca, a province farther north in present-day Kentucky. They were directed to search for a source of gold or silver. The scouts, however, found this land so inhospitable that de Soto decided against going into the region.

After two weeks, de Soto decided to leave. He asked the Indians for five hundred porters to help him. The Indians agreed, and de Soto left Chiaha on June 28, 1540, to march back into present-day northwestern Georgia.

Chapter 7

The End of the Expedition

De Soto arrived in the central village of Coosa on July 16, 1540. Coosa was located in the valley of the Coosawattee River, just east of present-day Cartersville, Georgia. All of the well-populated and successful chiefdoms the expedition had visited on its way from Chiaha paid homage to the powerful chief of the town of Coosa.

Coosa

Coosa was a kingdom with a territory more than two hundred miles long. It encompassed several river drainages in the lands that are found today in eastern Tennessee, northern Georgia, and east-central Alabama. The kingdom consisted of eleven to seventeen major villages and neighborhoods that were built along riverbanks. Each village controlled an area about thirteen miles in diameter—the approximate distance the chief could walk in one day.

The central village of Coosa was large. Probably more than three thousand people lived there when de Soto arrived.[1] There were three large mounds within the village. Usually, the houses of the principal citizens of a Mississippian Indian village were constructed on these earthen mounds. The Spaniards took over the homes on the mounds and the other principal homes of the village.[2]

Coosa had fields of corn that extended from the lands of one village to another. It was a land rich in fruits and vegetables. It reminded many of the Spaniards of the fertile areas of Spain. The Indians were wary of the Spaniards but were not overtly hostile. It was pleasant enough for the Spaniards, but it quickly became apparent that they would not find what they were looking for—hordes of gold or silver.

As a safeguard against a surprise Indian attack, de Soto usually took the chief of a province and held him hostage until the expedition had completed its march through his territory, at which point he would be released. On August 20, with fall quickly approaching, de Soto left Coosa, marching south to meet his supply ships, which were supposed to be waiting at Pensacola Bay. This time, he took as hostage not only the young chief of the Coosa, but also his sister. He kept them both in chains during the expedition's march south. The chief's sister would be the mother of the next chief of the Coosa. Her presence among the Spaniards was much more important to the Indians than the prince's.

As the expedition marched south through present-day northeastern Alabama, the news of de Soto's terrible tactics—such as taking hostages—preceded him. He began to meet opposition at every Indian village along the way. The prince of Coosa urged the angry villagers not to attack the Spaniards, fearing his life would be in danger.

The expedition finally reached the chiefdom of Talisi, the southernmost ally of Coosa. They rested there for almost three weeks. De Soto then released the prince of Coosa, but kept his sister prisoner. The prince begged de Soto to release the princess, but de Soto refused. This, on top of all the other humiliating demands the Spaniards had made led the ruling family of Coosa to decide to wage war on de Soto.

Kingdom of Tascaluza

Tascaluza was the next Mississippian chiefdom de Soto entered. The main chief of the land was also called Tascaluza. He was a giant of a man, fully six and a half feet tall. De Soto met the chief at his home near present-day Montgomery, Alabama. De Soto quickly put him in chains and forced him to march with the expedition when it left on October 12.

The Spaniards began to march through the wide prairie lands of central Alabama. Tascaluza told the Spaniards that they would find friendly women when they reached the town of Mabila. It was not women, however, who were waiting for them at the strongly fortified town of Mabila.

Battle of Mabila

In the early morning on October 18, 1540, Hernando de Soto and his advance guard, along with Chief Tascaluza, arrived at the village of Mabila, near present-day Selma, Alabama. The rest of the expedition trailed behind.

The village was located on an open plain that had been cleared by the Indians. There were no hiding places nearby. Even the bushes had been pulled up. The town was surrounded by a high, strongly fortified wall. There were two gates—one on the east side, the other on the west.

De Soto had learned in advance that the town was filled with warriors. There were no children or old

De Soto enters the town of Mabila, despite warnings that Chief Tascaluza was planning to ambush him there.

people, just young women and warriors. Tascaluza invited de Soto to either enter the town or remain outside. De Soto said he was tired of sleeping in the open country. Tying their horses outside one of the town's gates, de Soto and several members of his advance guard entered Tascaluza. They were shown to a shaded place that had been prepared for them.

All around, hundreds of young warriors watched. Twenty beautiful young Indian dancers entertained the Spaniards. Tascaluza then told de Soto that he no longer wanted to go along with the expedition. De Soto told him that he did not intend to leave him behind. Tascaluza got up and went inside a house near the square where they were sitting.

De Soto and Tascaluza met in Mabila, to discuss relations between the Spanish and Indians.

After a while, de Soto sent Baltasar de Gallegos into the house to get Tascaluza. The Indians inside attacked Gallegos when he entered. Luís de Moscoso, standing right outside, fought the Indians at the door and screamed for Gallegos to get out. The attack on Gallegos was a signal for the rest of the Indians in town to attack the Spaniards. Indian warriors poured out of all of the houses. De Soto and his men quickly headed for the gate. The Indians killed five of the Spaniards right away. All the others were wounded.

De Soto fell two or three times before he reached the gate but his guards protected him, and he survived. Gallegos and Moscoso, along with several others, fought their way all across the town and out the other gate. Two of de Soto's mounted guards, who had remained outside the town, rode up as he appeared. They held off about seventy Indian warriors with their lances as de Soto mounted a horse and took command.

The battle lasted all day long. It was a desperate struggle. Once all the combatants—both Indians and Spaniards—were outside the town, the heavily armored Spanish horses and lancers made the difference. Most of the three thousand Indians were forced back inside the village of Mabila. As soon as the main body of de Soto's expedition arrived at the scene, de Soto divided his men into four squadrons. The most heavily armored men, in the front, attacked the village walls, fighting off the Indian warriors while they hacked holes in the walls with axes. When the Spaniards finally entered the town, they set fire to

Although the Indian attack at Mabila took the Spaniards by surprise, it was the Indians who suffered the most casualties.

every house. The Indian warriors drove them out of town several times, but each time the Spaniards managed to fight their way back inside.

De Soto and one of his lieutenants, Nuño de Tovar, rode their horses through the town, spearing warriors to clear the streets for the incoming foot soldiers. De Soto was struck by an arrow in the buttock and had to fight standing up in his stirrups for several hours.

Thousands of Indians fought shoulder-to-shoulder to attack the armored Spaniards. Some Indians got out of the village, but most who tried to escape were hunted down and killed. Almost all the Indians—both men and women—fought wildly to the death. Hundreds died in the flaming houses. Those who were forced from the houses by the fires were killed in hand-to-hand combat. The last warrior left alive hanged himself with his bow string as a final act of defiance against the Spanish conquistadors. Probably close to three thousand Indians died that day. They were Indians from many different chiefdoms, some as far away as Coosa. For generations, their families told stories of their heroism that day, how they had avenged the many insults that had been heaped on them as the expedition passed through their lands.[3]

As night fell, everything in the Indian village, including the two hundred pounds of de Soto's pearls, burned. Twenty-two Spaniards had died, most with wounds to the face. De Soto's nephew, Captain Diego de Soto, had been shot through the eye by an arrow that penetrated the back of his skull. The 148 men who had been wounded averaged almost four wounds each. Seven horses had died and twenty-nine were wounded.

To Quit or Go On?

De Soto and his men rested at Mabila for almost a month. The expedition buried the dead. They were forced to treat the wounded with whatever they could find—their medicines had burned up along with the rest of de Soto's baggage. The men ate the dead horses and whatever else they could find within about ten miles. They burned whatever they could not eat.

While they were resting at Mabila, de Soto learned that Diego Maldonado, on the Spanish ship, was waiting for him at the port of Ochuse with his scheduled delivery of supplies. Maldonado had returned exactly on time. De Soto had planned and timed the giant loop around the Southeast perfectly. They were now just six days' travel—about a hundred miles—away from the supplies they so desperately needed.

The expedition had survived the battle of Mabila. It had won a glorious victory, but it had cost Hernando de Soto everything. He had found no gold or silver. He had lost his two hundred pounds of pearls. He had lost any proof that his expedition had been a success. Some of his friends, including his nephew, had died. In all, there had been 102 Spanish deaths during the journey, about one in six of the original expedition. The men were talking about de Soto's failure. There was even talk about how they might return to Spain or South America, where they could enjoy an easier, although less glamorous, life. De Soto had been a popular hero. He could not stand the possible humiliation he would receive if he returned to Spain as a failure. He preferred to die.

De Soto's crew crossed the Tombigee River in the autumn of 1540.

Instead of marching for his supplies and allowing the news of his failure to spread abroad, Hernando de Soto turned inland and marched away. De Soto rallied the men and led them northwest from Mabila on November 14, directly away from any contact or support. He led them back into the wilderness that promised no rewards and threatened death at every turn.

A Cold Winter Among the Chickasaw

De Soto marched northwest across Alabama and Mississippi. He had no reliable Indian guides. Instead, he sent his own men on scouting missions to find paths

The conquistadors tried to pursue the Chickasaw after the tribe attacked the expedition, killing several men.

and Indian villages where they could get new supplies. On November 30, 1540, de Soto met Apafalaya, an Indian who became a guide and interpreter. Apafalaya led the expedition through the forests and swamps to Chicasa, or the land of the Chickasaw people, in northern Mississippi.

The Chickasaw were living on the far side of the Tombigbee River. The expedition built rafts and crossed the river on December 17. By the time the Spaniards arrived, all the villagers had fled into the woods.

It was here in Chicasa that de Soto and his men spent the very cold winter of 1540–1541. The expedition was in sorry shape. By not going to meet his supply ships, de Soto had deprived the expedition of important supplies such as leather for new shoes, good cotton clothing, warm blankets, new swords, armor, guns, and gunpowder. The men were left to huddle inside the Chickasaw's village.

On March 4, 1541, the Chickasaw attacked and set fire to their village, catching the Spanish asleep. Twelve Spaniards died in the fires and the fight with the Indians. Most damaging, however, was the loss of the rest of the expedition's supplies. Nearly sixty of the remaining horses also died. De Soto wasted no time. The expedition pushed on immediately to escape the danger of another Indian attack.[4]

The Mississippi River

Every year, the overflow from the combined waters of the Ohio, Missouri, Arkansas, Red, and other rivers that emptied into the Mississippi River, renewed the soil and supported a vast population of humans and wildlife. In low-lying areas, water remained all year long, creating vast swamps.

The de Soto expedition marched eight days through the cold winter waters of several wilderness swamps to reach the chiefdom of Quizquiz near the present site of Memphis, Tennessee.[5] They quickly and peacefully moved through the villages of Quizquiz, eating whatever corn they found as well as large crops of a nut that was new to them—the pecan.

They camped on a high plain overlooking the wide Mississippi River below them to the west. Although the exact date is unknown, the Spaniards first saw the Mississippi River around May 15, 1541. They were the first Europeans to discover its broad expanse. It was the largest river any of them had ever seen.

De Soto was eager to cross to the other side. The men took twenty-seven days to cut trees and saw boards to construct some large, flat-bottomed boats.

Every day, Indian war canoes from the west side of the river came and threatened the expedition, shooting hundreds of arrows from a safe distance away. The Spaniards protected themselves with their shields and kept on working.

By June 18, the Spaniards had built four large flatboats. From where they were, the river was about a mile and a half wide and over a hundred feet deep. The current was very strong. Whole trees could be seen just zipping along downriver.

Shortly after midnight on the morning of June 18, the first boatloads of twelve horses and riders and about fifteen footmen were put into the water. The men rowed upstream for about a mile. Then they let the current take them, rowing energetically. They touched the opposite shore almost directly across from where they had pushed off. They had successfully crossed the Mississippi River. By the end of the morning, the entire expedition had been ferried across to present-day Arkansas.[6]

March Into Arkansas

Along the western side of the Mississippi River, the land was rich with cleared fields; small villages; and many pecan, mulberry, and persimmon trees. De Soto and his men entered the village of the Casqui on June 23. The expedition was in poor shape, so de Soto hoped he could maintain friendly relations with as many Indians as possible.

There had been no rain so far that summer, and a drought threatened the Indians' corn crop. De Soto had his carpenter erect a large wooden cross atop the highest mound in the village. Then he organized a huge procession to the foot of the cross, led by himself and the chief of the Casqui. That night, it rained steadily. The corn crop was saved. This fortunate turn of events helped begin an alliance. Together, the Spaniards and the Casqui waged war on one of the nearby enemies of the Casqui, the Pacaha. De Soto soon controlled both the Pacaha and Casqui leaders, both of whom sought him as an ally.

Giving up the Search for Gold

In July, de Soto sent thirty of his horsemen and fifty foot soldiers on an exploring party to the northwest. They reached a land of prairies where no trees grew. There was only grass. The Indians there lived in teepee-like pole houses covered with grass mats. There was little agriculture. Vast herds of buffalo roamed the land.

De Soto sent some of his men with trade goods to the north. They returned in about two weeks with crystals of salt that had been mined and some quantities of copper. To de Soto's great disappointment, they found no gold. In addition, the land was so poor that large crops of corn were unlikely. The expedition would likely starve if it went there.

De Soto led the expedition generally westward into the mountains of Arkansas. As he left the vicinity of the Mississippi River, the size and wealth of the Indian chiefdoms declined. The expedition began to give up its expectations of ever finding the gold and glory it had once envisioned. It moved on now driven simply by the pride that it could face any wilderness, any Indian, or any challenge.

The Spaniards were moving through unexplored, difficult terrain. The men had to survive by depending on each other. They had no shoes and no armor.

An artist painted this depiction of the death of Hernando de Soto on the banks of the river he was among the first Europeans to see.

These items had disintegrated in the forests, mountains, and swamps through which they had traveled.

On October 7, 1541, de Soto met the Tula Indians on the Arkansas River floodplain near present-day Fort Smith, Arkansas. Both the Tula men and women were fierce warriors. They were not afraid of the Spanish cavalry. They simply met the Spanish charge with their own long wooden lances. It was a technique they had learned facing down the charges of enraged buffalo. The Tula hunted buffalo, even in the winter, by wearing snowshoes. De Soto reluctantly came to a respectful peace with the Tula. From them, he learned that he would only find enough food for the coming winter if he traveled to the Southeast.

Death of the Conquistador

De Soto spent the very cold winter of 1541–1542 huddled in a Utiangüe Indian village on the Arkansas River near present-day Little Rock, Arkansas. It was so cold that the men of the expedition could stand to go outside only long enough to cut firewood. To make matters worse, during the winter, Juan Ortiz, the expedition's valued first interpreter, died. It was a terrible blow to the Spaniards.

On March 6, 1542, the men marched out of the Utiangüe village, down the Arkansas River toward its junction with the Mississippi River. The expedition now had fewer than four hundred men and fewer than forty horses left.

As de Soto approached the fertile Mississippi River floodplain, the chiefdoms were becoming larger and richer. The expedition passed into the lands of the Anilco and the Guachoya, two warring Mississippian chiefdoms who lived near the junction of the Mississippi and Arkansas rivers. De Soto learned that there were no large chiefdoms south on the western side of the Mississippi River. The land was nearly impassable, with vast swamps lying close to the river. He would not be able to return to the Gulf of Mexico that way.

Around April 25, 1542, de Soto fell ill with a fever that kept him in his bed. As days went by, he grew sicker. He soon realized that he was going to die. He gathered the royal representatives and his closest friends around him and thanked them for their loyalty, courage, and friendship. He asked them to elect a new leader for the expedition. They, however, wanted him to choose one of them to be the leader. De Soto nominated Luis de Moscoso, his friend and loyal lieutenant. The men of the expedition promptly elected Moscoso the captain-general to take them home. On May 21, 1542, Hernando de Soto died on the banks of the Mississippi River, which he and his men had been the first white people to see.

Effects of the Expedition

The Spaniards hid the body of Hernando de Soto for three days, and then buried the body near the wall of the village of Guachoya where they were staying. They did not want the Indians to know their leader had died. Many of the tribes believed de Soto was a god, and the Spaniards were afraid they would be brutally attacked if the Indians realized the truth.

The Indians of the village quickly noticed, however, that de Soto was missing. They also noticed the freshly turned dirt of the grave. Luis de Moscoso told the Indians that de Soto had gone back to heaven. Then, to prevent the Indians from investigating further, quietly dug up de Soto's body, weighed it down with loads of sand, and dropped it into the middle of the Mississippi River.

The members of the expedition turned to finding their way back to the nearest outpost of European civilization. They had two choices: They could travel

Source Document

The ceaseless howl of hungry wolves,
And known they were so near,
That as they fed the waning fires,
Their hearts were chilled with fear.

And all uncheered by jocund morn,
Haggard and hollow-eyed,
Awoke De Soto's weary band
By Mississippi's tide. . . .

Men of the proud Castilian race
Shed tears like summer rain,
Thinking of each familiar face
They ne'er might see again. . . .

And unfamiliar sounds of life
Came from the forest wild,
Scarce heeding them, De Soto lay,
As helpless as a child.

A priest without his holy guise
Said holy words to him,
And prayed that he in strength might rise
Yet still his eye grew dim;

And on his brow the dews of death
Were gathering thick and fast,
And with the morning's misty wreath,
Away his spirit passed.[1]

This poem commemorated the men's sadness at the death of Hernando de Soto.

overland to Mexico, which they knew was to the south-west; or they could build some boats, float down the Mississippi River to its mouth, and then sail either to Cuba or to Mexico. They were soldiers, not sailors, so they naturally chose to try to reach Mexico overland. It turned out to be a mistake.

The Long March Home

On June 5, 1542, the expedition began its march to Mexico. The men moved south and southwest across present-day Arkansas and Texas. The farther they went, the poorer were the Indian chiefdoms. There was less and less food to eat.

The survivors of the de Soto expedition had to withstand Indian attacks as they built ships to sail home.

As they traveled south through the pine forests of east Texas, they made contact with the Caddo people. The Caddo were not a Mississippian culture, and even though they farmed a little corn, the Spaniards realized that there would not be enough Indian corn along their route to keep them alive all the way to Mexico.

The land was becoming open, with large expanses of prairies extending to the horizon. The climate was also getting hotter, and there was little water to be found. The Spaniards were approaching the arid lands that Cabeza de Vaca had described to de Soto, a land where the Indians had no towns, but instead wandered around searching for food from the cactus plants, roots, and nuts they found.

The expedition finally reached what they called the river of Daycao, which may have been the Colorado River. The men decided that they would starve if they continued on this route. In October 1542, they turned around and began to retrace their steps. In December, they reached the Mississippi River again.

Now they decided to try the plan they had initially rejected: to sail down the Mississippi and out to sea. They soon began to build seven boats to take them down the river. The boats were finished in June 1543.

On July 2, 1543, the men started down the Mississippi River toward the Gulf of Mexico. It was a trip of seven hundred fifty miles.

The current was strong, and the men quickly passed thousands of Indians in giant war canoes. For several days, they were under constant attack. When they passed present-day Natchez, Mississippi, the Indian attacks stopped. They had traveled beyond the last large chiefdom located along the river.

Pedro Menéndez de Aviles founded the city of St. Augustine, Florida, which is now the oldest continual settlement in what is now the United States.

Source Document

The next morning, being fully persuaded that the storm had made a wreck of our galley, or that, at least, she had been driven a hundred leagues out to sea, we decided that as soon as daylight came we would weigh anchor and withdraw to a river which was below the French colony, and there disembark, and construct a fort, which we would defend until assistance came to us.

Our fort is at a distance of about fifteen leagues from that of the enemy. The energy and talents of these two brave captains, joined to the efforts of their brave soldiers, who had no tools with which to work the earth, accomplished the construction of this fortress of defense; and, when the general disembarked, he was quite surprised with what had been done.[2]

Francisco López de Mendoza Grajales gave this account of the founding of the city of St. Augustine.

It took twelve more days to reach the mouth of the river and sail out into the Gulf of Mexico. The Spaniards turned toward the west and followed the coast.

Finally, on September 10, 1543, they reached the mouth of the Pánuco River near the city of Veracruz, Mexico. It had been four years and four months since they left Cuba. They had marched approximately thirty-five hundred miles across North America. About half of the members of the expedition survived.

Further Spanish Exploration

The Spanish government remained interested in the lands around the coast of the Gulf of Mexico after the end of the de Soto expedition, even though the exploration had found no rich sources of gold.[3] In the summer of 1559, Tristán de Luna y Arellano led an expedition of thirteen ships and fifteen hundred people to the Gulf coast of Florida. He landed at Tampa Bay and soon moved to Pensacola Bay. De Luna sent about one hundred fifty men under the command of Mateo del Sauz on a foraging expedition to find Coosa, the inland chiefdom that de Soto had found so rich in food. After almost two months of travel, del Sauz's men reached the towns of Coosa. The entire area had suffered much since the time of de Soto's passage a generation before. What had been a rich and densely populated kingdom was now poor. There were fewer villages, less food, and fewer people. Some of the Spaniards were convinced that they had come to the wrong place.[4]

King Philip II of Spain carried on de Soto's legacy, establishing colonies in North America.

In 1565, a Spanish fleet under the command of Pedro Menéndez de Avilés came to the Atlantic coast of Georgia to destroy a French settlement that had been established there the year before. He established the town of St. Augustine in northern Florida, in September 1565. This would be the first permanent settlement in what would become the United States. His superior forces quickly routed the French. Then, he established another settlement at Santa Elena in the spring of 1566 and other outposts along the Florida and Georgia coasts.

A Deadly Legacy

Beginning in 1568, Spanish missionaries who hoped to convert the Indians to Christianity began to establish Catholic churches among the Tequesta and Calusa Indians in south Florida and the Guale and Orista Indians of Georgia. By the 1650s, these churches, or missions, had also been established in the land of the Apalachee in western Florida. In all, there were some forty Spanish missions, serving about fifteen thousand Indians in Florida and Georgia.

Unfortunately, the missionary efforts of the Spanish took a terrible toll on the Indians of the Southeast. Diseases carried by the missionaries and other Europeans, to which the Indians had no immunity, nearly wiped out most of the tribes in Florida. Epidemics of measles, mumps, malaria, smallpox, typhoid, typhus, influenza, yellow fever, and bubonic plague that periodically swept through the region had killed almost everyone. When a disease began to kill the members of an Indian village, many families simply ran away from the settled areas into the forest wilderness, hoping to escape the deadly epidemic.

What had once been a mainly uninhabited wilderness between the large Mississippian chiefdoms now began to house small groups of Indian families. Whole villages moved away from their former locations to escape disease. Many villages formed new alliances, and even new tribes. The peoples of the Coosa and the Talisi as well as refugees from other tribes, for example, formed an alliance and became known as the Upper Creek.[5] East central Mississippi became the center of an alliance of several former chiefdoms of the area in the seventeenth century. It was known as the Choctaw alliance. In the mountains of North Carolina and Tennessee, the Cherokee managed to remain together largely through shrewd alliances with various European nations and other Indian tribes.

As they, too, set up American colonies, the English raided these tribes for slaves, sold the Cherokee guns, and periodically attacked villages, killing as many Indians as they found. Along with the devastating effects of disease, these problems vastly decreased the population of Indian natives. By the time the new United States of America won England's former territories after the American Revolution ended in 1783, there were no more Mississippian societies left in the Southeast. Over the next few decades, the Americans would drive away all the Indians still living in the Southeast west across the Mississippi River, in order to open the area to settlement by white citizens.

Since de Soto first arrived, everything has changed, including the Mississippi River. Today, through the creation of dams and spillways, the Mississippi no longer overflows its banks every year to create the

Hernando de Soto's discovery of the Mississippi, the largest river in North America, opened an important trade route to European colonists.

fertile floodplains that once nurtured huge crops of Indian corn. The Mississippi has become a dependable highway, filled with barges and ships bringing the goods of the heartland of America to the port city of New Orleans, Louisiana, for shipment all over the world. It is no longer the same wonder-filled wilderness that de Soto and his men saw, surrounded by the great Mississippi chiefdoms. In fact, no European ever saw those thriving cultures again.

De Soto's legacy is a mixed one. His brave trek through the untamed wilds of southeastern America broadened the European view of the world's geography, and also opened the valuable trade route of the Mississippi River. In carrying out his relentless search for gold, however, he and the other Europeans who followed him destroyed entire civilizations that can never be replaced.

Timeline

1492—Christopher Columbus reaches islands in the Caribbean, claiming the lands of the Americas for Spain.

1500—Hernando de Soto born in Extremadura, Spain.

1514—De Soto sails to Panama with the Pedrarias Dávila expedition.

1519—De Soto becomes a field captain in Juan de Espinosa's conquest of western Panama.

1524—De Soto serves as field captain in Córdoba's conquest of Nicaragua.

1528—De Soto becomes a wealthy landowner in Nicaragua.

1531—De Soto takes part in Francisco Pizarro's conquest of the Inca of Peru.

1536—De Soto returns to Spain a famous and very wealthy conquistador.

1537—Emperor Charles V gives de Soto a contract to conquer North America.

1538—The de Soto expedition leaves Spain for Cuba.

1539—*May 25:* De Soto lands at Tampa Bay, Florida, to begin his adventures.

1539—De Soto spends the winter at Apalachee.
–1540

1540—*October 18:* Battle of Mabila takes place.

1540—De Soto winters at Chicasa.
–1541

1541—*March 4:* Battle of Chicasa takes place.

> *c. May 15:* De Soto sights the Mississippi River for the first time.

1541—De Soto winters at Utiangüe on the
–1542   Arkansas River.

1542—*May 21:* De Soto dies near the Mississippi River; Luis de Moscoso leads expedition overland toward Mexico.

1542—Expedition winters near Guachoya on the
–1543   Mississippi River.

1543—*July 2:* Expedition sails down Mississippi River to Gulf of Mexico.

> *September 10:* Expedition arrives at Veracruz, Mexico.

Chapter Notes

Chapter 1. The Landing

1. Jerald T. Milanich, *Florida Indians and the Invasion From Europe* (Gainesville: University Press of Florida, 1995), p. 129.

2. Bartolomé de las Casas, "Spanish Atrocities in the West Indies, c. 1513–20," *Eyewitness to History,* ed. John Carey (New York: Avon Books, 1987), p. 82.

3. Charles Hudson, *Knights of Spain, Warriors of the Sun: Hernando de Soto and the South's Ancient Chiefdoms* (Athens: University of Georgia Press, 1998), p. 80.

4. Lawrence A. Clayton, Vernon James Knight, Jr., and Edward C. Moore, eds., *The De Soto Chronicles: The Expedition of Hernando de Soto to North America in 1539–1543* (Tuscaloosa: University of Alabama Press, 1995), vol. 2, pp. 101–104.

Chapter 2. The Indians of North America

1. Charles Hudson and Carmen Tesser, eds., *The Forgotten Centuries: Indians and Europeans in the American South 1521–1704* (Athens: University of Georgia Press, 1994), p. 18.

2. Charles Hudson, *Knights of Spain, Warriors of the Sun: Hernando de Soto and the South's Ancient Chiefdoms* (Athens: University of Georgia Press, 1998), p. 154.

3. James A. Maxwell, ed., *America's Fascinating Indian Heritage* (Pleasantville, N.Y.: Reader's Digest Association, Inc., 1978), p. 34.

4. Ibid., p. 41.

5. Ibid., pp. 39–40.

6. Jon Manchip White, *Everyday Life of the North American Indians* (New York: Holmes & Meier Publishers, 1979), p. 65.

7. Charles Hudson, *The Southeastern Indians* (Knoxville, Tenn.: University of Tennessee Press, 1976), p. 80.

8. Alvin M. Josephy, Jr., *500 Nations: An Illustrated History of North American Indians* (New York: Knopf, 1994), pp. 40–41; James A. Maxwell, ed., *America's Fascinating Indian Heritage, p. 70; Charles Hudson, Knights of Spain, Warriors of the Sun: Hernando de Soto and the South's Ancient Chiefdoms,* pp. 24–25.

9. Charles Hudson, *Knights of Spain, Warriors of the Sun: Hernando de Soto and the South's Ancient Chiefdoms,* p. 12.

Chapter 3. The Spanish in America

1. Robert Silverberg, *The Golden Dream: Seekers of El Dorado* (Athens: Ohio University Press, 1996), p. 139.

2. Christopher Columbus, "Columbus Reaches the Americas, Bahamas, 12 October 1492," *The Mammoth Book of Eye-Witness History,* ed. Jon E. Lewis (New York: Carroll & Graf Publishers, 1998), p. 97.

3. John H. Parry and Robert G. Keith, eds., *New Iberian World: A Documentary History of the Discovery and Settlement of Latin America to the Early 17th Century* (New York: Times Books, 1984), vol. 2, p. 222.

4. David Ewing Duncan, *Hernando de Soto: A Savage Quest in the Americas* (New York: Crown Publishers, 1995), pp. 5–9.

5. Jerald T. Milanich, Laboring in the Fields of the Lord, Spanish Missions and Southeastern Indians (Washington: Smithsonian Institution Press, 1999), p. 33.

6. Paul E. Hoffman, "Introduction: The De Soto Expedition, a Cultural Crossroads," in *The De Soto Chronicles,* 2 vols., ed. Lawrence Clayton (Tuscaloosa: University of Alabama Press, 1990), vol. 1, p. 2.

Chapter 4. De Soto's Early Career

1. Paul E. Hoffman, "Hernando De Soto: A Brief Biography," in *The De Soto Chronicles,* 2 vols., ed. Lawrence A. Clayton (Tuscaloosa: The University of Alabama Press, 1993), vol. 1, p. 423.

2. John H. Parry and Robert G. Keith, eds., *New Iberian World,* 5 vols. (New York: Times Books and Hector & Rose, 1984), vol. 3, p. 49.

3. David Ewing Duncan, *Hernando de Soto: A Savage Quest in the Americas* (New York: Crown Publishers, 1995), pp. 60–63; Hoffman, "Hernando De Soto: A Brief Biography," pp. 424–426.

4. Parry and Keith, pp. 86–89.

5. Garcilaso de la Vega, "The Incas' Golden Garden," *Eyewitness to History,* ed. John Carey (New York: Avon Books, 1987), p. 89.

6. "Concession made by the King of Spain to Hernando de Soto of the Government of Cuba and Conquest of Florida, with the title of Adelantado," Clayton, vol. 1, p. 365.

Chapter 5. The Expedition Begins

1. Jerald T. Milanich and Susan Milbrath, eds., *First Encounters: Spanish Explorations in the Caribbean and the United States, 1492–1570* (Gainesville: University Press of Florida, 1989), p. 53; for illustrations of how they were transported, p. 125.

2. Charles Hudson, *Knights of Spain, Warriors of the Sun: Hernando de Soto and the South's Ancient Chiefdoms* (Athens: University of Georgia Press, 1998), p. 74.

3. Lawrence A. Clayton, Vernon James Knight, Jr., and Edward C. Moore, eds., *The De Soto Chronicles: The Expedition of Hernando de Soto to North America in 1539–1543* (Tuscaloosa: University of Alabama Press, 1995), vol. 1, pp. 366–371, 373.

Chapter 6. The Expedition to Mabila

1. Charles Hudson, *Knights of Spain, Warriors of the Sun: Hernando de Soto and the South's Ancient Chiefdoms* (Athens: University of Georgia Press, 1998), pp. 90, 105 ff.

2. Ibid., p. 103.

3. Alvin M. Josephy, Jr., *500 Nations: An Illustrated History of North American Indians* (New York: Knopf, 1994), p. 146.

4. Ibid., p. 148.

Chapter 7. The End of the Expedition

1. Charles Hudson, *Knights of Spain, Warriors of the Sun: Hernando de Soto and the South's Ancient Chiefdoms* (Athens: University of Georgia Press, 1998), p. 215.

2. Ibid., p. 218.

3. Ibid., pp. 232–240.

4. Charles Hudson, "Hernando de Soto," pp. 89–90.

5. Hudson, *Knights of Spain,* pp. 275–278.

6. Ibid., pp. 278–286.

Chapter 8. Effects of the Expedition

1. J.B.P., "The Death of Hernando de Soto," *The United States Democratic Review,* vol. 8, issue 32, August 1840, pp. 174–176.

2. Francisco López de Mendoza Grajales, "The Founding of St. Augustine," *Eyewitness to America: 500 Years of America in the Words of Those Who Saw It Happen,* ed. David Colbert (New York: Pantheon Books, 1997), p. 10.

3. Gloria A. Young and Michael P. Hoffman, eds., *The Expedition of Hernando de Soto West of the Mississippi,*

1541–1543 (Fayetteville: The University of Arkansas Press, 1993), pp. 23–24.

4. Jerald T. Milanich and Susan Milbrath, eds., *First Encounters: Spanish Explorations in the Caribbean and the United States, 1492–1570* (Gainesville: University of Florida Press, 1989), pp. 130–134.

5. Jerald T. Milanich and Susan Milbrath, eds., *First Encounters,* pp. 140–142.

Further Reading

Duncan, David E. *Hernando de Soto: A Savage Quest in the Americas.* New York: Crown Publishers, Inc., 1995.

Galagher, Jim. *Hernando De Soto and the Exploration of Florida.* Philadelphia: Chelsea House Publishers, 2000.

Kennedy, Roger C. *Hidden Cities: The Discovery and Loss of Ancient North American Civilization.* New York: Free Press, 1994.

Larkin, Tanya. *Hernando De Soto: The Stubborn Conquistador.* New York: PowerKids Press, 2001.

Sanchez, Richard. *Explorers and Conquerors.* Edina, Minn.: Abdo & Daughters, 1994.

Whitman, Sylvia. *Hernando De Soto and the Explorers of the American South.* New York: Chelsea House Publishers, 1991.

Internet Addresses

The Applied History Research Group. "The European Voyages of Exploration." *University of Calgary.* July 5, 2001. <http://www.ucalgary.ca/applied_history/tutor/eurvoya/>.

"De Soto National Memorial." *National Park Service.* September 8, 2001. <http://www.nps.gov/deso/>.

Sheppard, Donald E. "Hernando de Soto's Trails Through North America." *Native American Conquest Corporation.* 2000. <http://www.vaca.com/inset44.html>.

"The Soto Expedition." *Archeology, Inc.* n.d. <http://www.archeologyinc.org/soto.html>.

Index